EMERGING LOYALTIES

JACK CECILLON
PINA SACCO
CRAIG ZIMMER

DATE DUE

CANADA
A PEOPLE'S HISTORY

THOMSON

NELSON

Australia   Canada   Mexico   Singapore   Spain   United Kingdom   United States

THOMSON

NELSON

Canada: A People's History
Emerging Loyalties

Series Consultants
Donald Bogle, Don Quinlan

Author
Jack Cecillon, Pina Sacco, Craig Zimmer

Director of Publishing
Beverley Buxton

General Manager, Social Studies, Business Studies, and Languages
Carol Stokes

Publisher, Social Studies
Doug Panasis

Managing Editor, Development
Karin Fediw

Product Manager
Nadia McIlveen

Senior Editor
Susan Petersiel Berg

Editorial Coordinator
Amy Hingston

Executive Director, Content and Media Production
Renate McCloy

Director, Content and Media Production
Lisa Dimson

Production Manager
Cathy Deak

Senior Production Coordinator
Kathrine Pummell

Interior and Cover Design
Daniel Crack, Kinetics Design

Photo Research
Lisa Brant, Alene McNeill

Printer
Transcontinental Printing Inc.

Canadian Broadcasting Corporation Representative
Karen Bower

The authors and the publisher are grateful to the Canadian Broadcasting Corporation for its assistance in the preparation of this volume in the book series based on its 17-episode, bilingual television documentary series, *Canada: A People's History*. For more information about *Canada: A People's History*, please visit www.cbc.ca/history.

Canada: A People's History
© 2000, 2001 Canadian Broadcasting Corporation

Contents

INTRODUCTION

THE BIG IDEA

Most Canadians are proud to live in a country that is **bilingual**. Have you ever wondered why we have two official languages?

Three hundred years ago, the world's most powerful empires, France and Britain, clashed on Canadian soil. The two countries and their Native allies fought for power and territory. Their victories and losses helped shape the Canada we live in today.

Canada is often praised for being a tolerant and peaceful society. Today, it has a reputation as a country that supports the United Nations and its attempts to make the world less violent. Canadian history, however, has been full of violence. The battle depicted in this picture, *A View of the Taking of Quebec, 1759*, is central to understanding why Canada is bilingual and why it did not become part of the United States.

TIMELINE

1605 French colony established at Port Royal in Acadia

1608 Founding of Quebec City

1663 King Louis XIV takes control of New France

1755 French defeat British at Fort Duquesne Acadians deported

1756–1763 Britain and France wage Seven Years' War

1607 British colony established in Virginia, first of the Thirteen Colonies

1642 Founding of Montreal

1683 War breaks out between Britain and France

1713 Treaty of Utrecht: France surrenders Acadia to Britain

Native trappers with a birchbark canoe. The canoe's light weight and shallow body made it ideal for travelling in both deep and shallow water and for carrying, or portaging, from one river to the next.

PICTURE THIS

Imagine Canada as the New World, when it was known only to the First Nations people who lived there. Across the ocean, Britain and France struggle to expand their empires and send explorers to this new place. The explorers meet the First Nations who live on the land. They kill many Native people and befriend others who teach them how to survive. France and Britain move their quest for more land and power to the New World. They establish colonies and claim territory that belongs to the First Nations. They battle each other for control of North America.

What part did the three founding peoples of Canada—the British, the French, and the First Nations—play in our country's early history? Why does Canada have two official languages? Why does the Province of Quebec have its own legal code?

TIMELINE

1758 France surrenders Fort Louisbourg to Britain

1760 New France becomes a British colony

1765 Chief Pontiac signs peace agreement with British

1775 American rebels attack Quebec

1759 British defeat French on Plains of Abraham

1763 Treaty of Paris Proclamation Act

1774 Quebec Act

1776 Thirteen Colonies declare independence from Britain

Why do some people in Quebec want their province to become a separate country? What do past battles between Britain and France have to do with Canada today?

SETTING THE SCENE

The Last Days of New France

By 1750, descendants of French settlers had been living in the New World for almost 150 years. Because they had been born in Canada, they were called *Canadiens*. Most were farmers, or *habitants*, who worked long, narrow strips of land that began at the banks of the St. Lawrence and Richelieu rivers. They were the people of New France, which was an important piece of the French empire.

Further south, along the Atlantic coast, were the Thirteen Colonies. They were younger than the French colonies and belonged to the British empire. The people were mostly Protestant, and saw the Catholic colony of New France as competition in the fur trade. The only way to prosper, they thought, was to drive the French out.

Louis Hébert was the first farmer in New France. Within 150 years, there were 10 000 *habitant* farmers.

Canada: Land of Many Languages

Canada has always been a land of many different languages. Long before European settlers arrived, the First Nations spoke dozens of languages. As the English and French fought for control of the New World, they ignored the language traditions of the First Nations. They wanted to build communities that were like the ones they had left behind. Today, Canada is a bilingual country, but there are still clashes over language rights.

Battles between France and Britain

For 150 years, power in North America shifted back and forth between the French and the English. They fought many battles to win control of the New World, often with the First Nations as **allies**. The most important battle was also the shortest. The battle at the **Plains of Abraham** in 1759 between the French forces of General Montcalm and the British forces of General Wolfe lasted only 15 minutes, but it shaped the country, the languages, and the laws that are part of Canada today.

Scottish Highlanders, part of the British forces at the Plains of Abraham, scale a cliff before the battle.

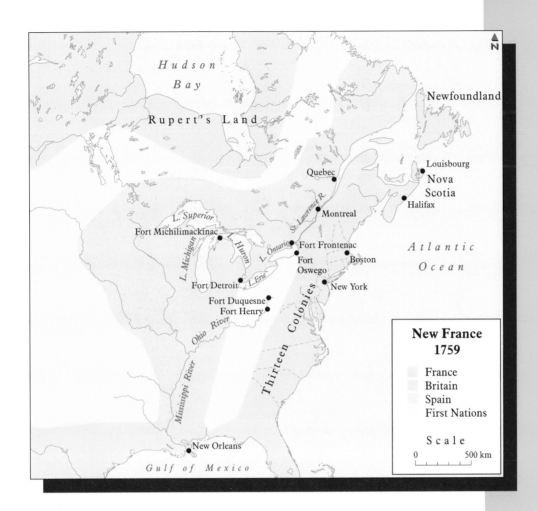

The map shows the following labels: Hudson Bay, Rupert's Land, Newfoundland, Louisbourg, Nova Scotia, Halifax, Quebec, Montreal, L. Superior, Fort Michilimackinac, L. Huron, L. Michigan, L. Ontario, Fort Frontenac, Fort Oswego, Boston, St. Lawrence R., Fort Detroit, L. Erie, New York, Fort Duquesne, Fort Henry, Ohio River, Atlantic Ocean, Thirteen Colonies, Mississippi River, New Orleans, Gulf of Mexico

New France 1759

France
Britain
Spain
First Nations

Scale
0   500 km

The Quebec Act and the American Revolution

Once Britain had control of the continent, it also had control over the French-Catholic *Canadiens*, who struggled to survive under British rule. The new governor of the colony, Guy Carleton, was sympathetic. He pushed for the passage of the Quebec Act in 1774 to protect the rights of the *Canadiens*.

To the south of Quebec, rebellion was already brewing in the Thirteen Colonies. More and more people were demanding significant changes in the way Britain governed the colonies. For them, the Quebec Act—with its special rights for *Canadiens*—was the last straw. It turned out to be one of the sparks that set off the American Revolution. When the revolution ended in 1783, the Thirteen Colonies were the independent country of the United States. Britain had lost America, but continued to rule over Canada.

Two Languages Today

In 1969, the government of Prime Minister Pierre Trudeau passed the Official Languages Act, which made Canada a bilingual country of French and English. The law does not force everyone in the country to become fluent in both official languages. It means that any Canadian should be able to communicate with the government by mail, in person, or on the phone in either English or French. All official documents, such as tax forms and government reports, must be available in both languages.

The Canadian Coat of Arms has many symbols that represent Canada's past and present. Across the bottom is Canada's national motto, "A Mari Usque ad Mare" ("From Sea to Sea").

◀Playback▶

1. **What languages do you speak?**

2. **What evidence do you see in everyday life that Canada is a bilingual nation? In your view, what are the advantages and disadvantages of living in a bilingual nation?**

3. **Analyse Canada's coat of arms.**

   (a) **List the symbols that represent our ties to other nations.**

   (b) **Which symbol is used to represent Canada today?**

   (c) **Are there symbols missing from any of the founding peoples? Why do you think they have been forgotten?**

4. **Design a coat of arms that represents all three founding peoples of Canada. Include a short explanation of your choice of symbols.**

BATTLING FOR NEW FRANCE

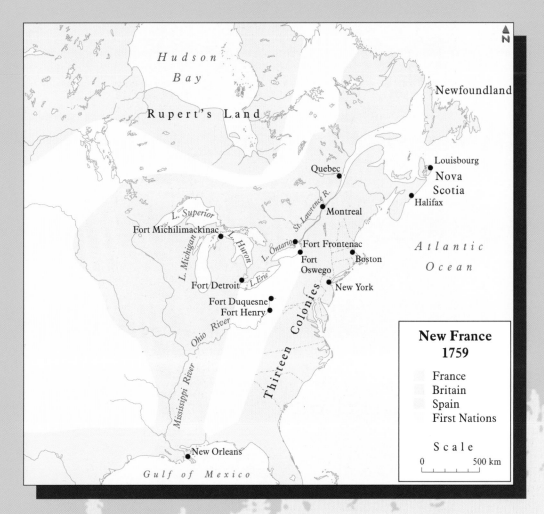

Hudson
Bay

Rupert's Land

Newfoundland

Quebec

Louisbourg
Nova
Scotia
Halifax

L. Superior

St. Lawrence R.

Montreal

Fort Michilimackinac

L. Michigan

L. Huron

L. Ontario

Fort Frontenac

Atlantic
Ocean

Fort
Oswego

Boston

Fort Detroit

L. Erie

Fort Duquesne
Fort Henry

Ohio River

New York

Thirteen Colonies

Mississippi River

New Orleans

Gulf of Mexico

**New France
1759**

France
Britain
Spain
First Nations

Scale

0   500 km

NEW FRANCE

In 1758, New France occupied a vast territory in North America. It began
at **Louisbourg**, ran along the St. Lawrence River, stretched beyond the
Great Lakes, and extended south down the Mississippi River to New
Orleans. About 55 000 people lived in the French colony, most of them
in old, established settlements along the St. Lawrence River.

Quebec City, which had been founded in 1608, was the capital of
New France. The city was a bustling centre of almost 8000 people, and
contained Catholic churches and schools, shops, warehouses, and markets.
It was an important port for the furs going out of the colony and the supplies and settlers coming in from France. Military forces occupied the
fortress that had been built above the river. The **King's Road** ran west
from Quebec City to Montreal. Montreal was home to about 5000 people
and the headquarters of the French fur trade.

THE *CANADIENS*

The *Canadiens* lived along the St. Lawrence River, and could trace their ancestry back to Samuel de Champlain's settlers in the early 1600s. Most were farmers, or *habitants*, who grew crops and raised livestock on long, narrow strips of land along the river. Their farms belonged to **seigneurs**, privileged men who had received the land grants from the king of France. The *habitants* paid rent by giving part of their annual harvest to the *seigneur*. They were also expected to work a few days each year repairing community roads and bridges. The *habitants* counted on help from the *seigneur*. He ran the mill where they ground their wheat into flour. When there was a disagreement, the *seigneur* acted as a judge. If children were orphaned, he found a family to look after them. In times of war, he protected the *habitants*, who were expected to volunteer in the militia.

La Petite Guerre

The *Canadiens* were skilled in the techniques of Native warfare. They knew how to creep silently through the woods and launch surprise attacks. This fighting style, called ***la petite guerre***, impressed the Marquis de Vaudreuil, the first governor of New France. He instructed his own militia to use it in battle. The French launched frequent attacks on the British colonies and usually won.

The Horse Trader was one of many paintings by Cornelius Krieghoff that captured the daily lives of the *Canadiens*.

FIRST NATIONS

The French had close ties with First Nations people that dated back to the early 1600s and the days of Champlain. Native people had taught early French explorers and settlers how to survive the harsh winters, when many were dying of scurvy, a disease caused by a lack of vitamin C. They had introduced fur traders to the birchbark canoe and snowshoes so they could navigate through the wilderness.

Indian Hunters by Cornelius Krieghoff

The success of the French fur trade depended on Native hunters. They brought their beaver pelts to the French fur posts and traded them for knives, kettles, blankets, and beads. They guided the ***coureurs de bois*** through fur-trading territories. The *coureurs de bois* learned Native languages, and many married Native women, strengthening the ties between the *Canadiens* and the First Nations.

Alliances

The French needed to keep a strong alliance with the Algonquin, Huron, and Montagnais nations to ensure a steady supply of furs. In return, the French agreed to help them defend themselves against the Iroquois. After French forces defeated the Iroquois in several battles, the Iroquois nation became an arch-enemy. Through the 1600s, the Iroquois attacked both their Native enemies and French settlements, including Montreal.

By the mid-1700s, a clash between France and Britain seemed inevitable. Britain's Hudson's Bay Company was moving in on the fur trade to the north of French territory, and the British colonies along the Atlantic coast were eyeing French territory in the Ohio River valley.

The King's Gifts

As the fur trade expanded, the French needed to build more forts that were closer to the Native trappers. First Nations granted them permission to build forts on Native land. In exchange, the king of France began a tradition of annual gift giving. Once a year, French military commanders stationed at fur-trading posts welcomed First Nations chiefs. They were presented with gifts from the king—fine cloth, **muskets**, **black powder** and ammunition, tin pots, and tools. These gifts were special to the Native people because they were available only from the king, and not from regular trade at the post. The celebrations that followed lasted the entire day and ended with Native dances of thanksgiving.

Coming Storm at the Portage
by Cornelius Krieghoff

THE BRITISH COLONIES

In the 1600s, many British settlers, most of them Protestant, had come to the New World. Some were escaping religious persecution. Others were looking for land to farm. Some came to make money. Another group dreamed of creating a perfect world of freedom, equality, and opportunity for all people—as long as they were English.

In the 1750s, Britain's colonies in North America did not occupy as much land as France's colonies, but they had many more people. More than one million people lived in the Thirteen Colonies, which ran down the Atlantic coast. To the north, the British colonies were smaller but well established. About 9000 people lived in the colony of Nova Scotia, and about 7000 people lived in the colony of Newfoundland. This region also contained 10 000 French-speaking **Acadians**, who had come under British rule in 1713.

Back in Britain, many merchants hoped to make their fortunes in the New World. They sent shiploads of slaves, firearms, nails, furniture, and rum to the colonies. The ships returned to England loaded with tobacco, lumber, and beaver pelts. The British had already driven the Swedish and the Dutch out of the New World in their quest for furs. All that stood in the way of British control of the fur trade were the settlers of New France and a few thousand French soldiers.

THE IROQUOIS CONFEDERACY

The British formed a military alliance with the Iroquois Confederacy, a group made up of five First Nations peoples: Mohawk, Seneca, Cayuga, Onondaga, and Oneida. In 1722, the Tuscaroras joined the confederacy.

The Iroquois Confederacy had a system of government that included elected representatives who made decisions for the villages and bands. To make sure that every nation had a say in important matters, each elected representatives to the Great Council, which made decisions about the whole confederacy. Later, when the Americans created their own government, they copied the system of the Iroquois Confederacy.

A British trader speaks to a council of Iroquois warriors

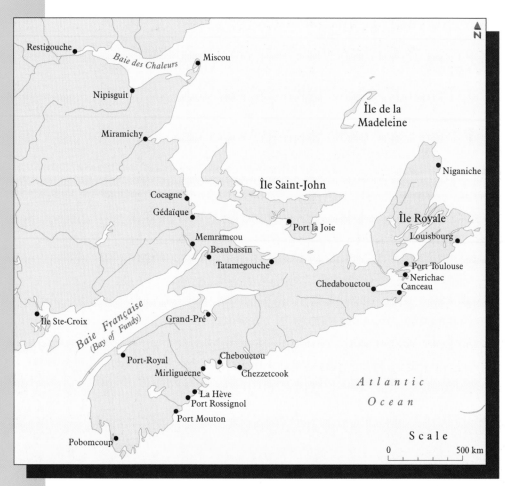

Acadia, 1750

THE BOILING POINT

In 1755, trouble erupted in North America on several fronts. The tension between the British and French was about to boil over.

The Acadians

Acadia was part of the maritime region on the Atlantic coast, which now includes the provinces of New Brunswick, Nova Scotia, and Prince Edward Island. The French first established a settlement there in 1603. Settlers built their homes around the Bay of Fundy and lived in harmony with the local Native people, the Mi'kmaq. The most serious threat to the Acadians was continuing hostility between France and Britain. Within 100 years, control of Acadia passed from the French to the British and back again at least six times. Britain finally conquered Acadia for good in 1713.

By the early 1750s, the Acadian population had reached almost 13 000. The British worried that, if Britain and France declared war, the French-speaking Catholics of Acadia would turn against the British. They asked the Acadians to swear an oath of loyalty to the king of England. The king was not just the head of the state; he was also the head of the Anglican Church of England. The Catholic Acadians refused to swear an oath of loyalty to the head of the Anglican Church.

Deportation of the Acadians

By 1755, Britain and France were on the brink of war in Europe. Once again, the British demanded that the Acadians swear an oath of allegiance to the king of England. Again, they refused. King George ordered British troops to drive the Acadians off their land and **deport** them to make way for British settlers. Between 1755 and 1763, the British expelled thousands of Acadians from their homes. One-third of them died from disease, hunger, and exhaustion as they searched for new places to live. Some found their way back to France. Some escaped to Canada. Some hid in the woods. A large number found their way to Louisiana. Today, French-speaking Cajuns can trace their ancestry to the refugees of Acadia.

In 1755, the British expelled 8000 Acadians from their homes.

Trouble on the Western Frontier

By the 1750s, a crisis was also brewing between the French and British in the Ohio River valley, an unsettled **frontier** west of the Thirteen Colonies. It was an important part of France's fur-trading territory. King Louis XV of France depended on furs from this western territory to pay for his armies in Europe. He built forts in the area to protect his fur-trading lands and the roads leading to the fur-trading centres of Montreal and Quebec City.

As more British settlers in the Thirteen Colonies bought farms, a land shortage developed. Settlers and colonial officials started looking at the land further west—at the fur-trading territory that belonged to the French. When British merchants sold land in the Ohio River valley to a group of Virginia businessmen, the French claimed that the land belonged to them.

The French built more forts in the area, including Fort Duquesne, near present-day Pittsburgh. They continued to raid new British settlements. Fearing for their lives, British colonists abandoned their farms and fled to towns on the east coast. Soon the towns were overcrowded, and people faced sickness and

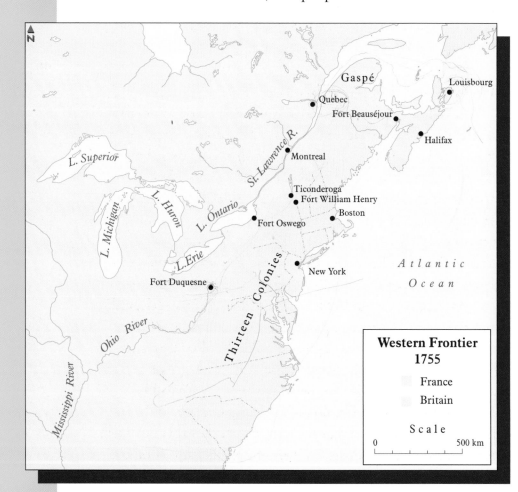

The defeat of General Braddock and his British forces in 1755

starvation. To encourage the settlers to join the army, newspapers printed exaggerated tales of cruel attacks by First Nations peoples and their French allies. Tensions mounted.

Flashpoint: Fort Duquesne

In 1754, the British governor of Virginia ordered Lieutenant Colonel George Washington to attack Fort Duquesne and seize it from the French. Marching in two long rows, dressed in their brilliant red uniforms, the British attacked. The soldiers were trained to fight the way they fought on the battlefields in Europe —each row taking a turn firing and then kneeling to reload. They were no match for the French army, aided by the *Canadien* militia and their Native allies, who fired on the British columns from behind bushes, trees, and hills. Washington's army was defeated.

The next year, the British launched another attack on Fort Duquesne. Hoping to surprise the French forces, General Braddock led his men through swamplands. When French and Native snipers began shooting at the British troops, they were unable to defend themselves because their muskets and gunpowder were wet. The British forces panicked, and Braddock had no choice but to retreat. After their victory, the French were convinced that defeating the British was only a matter of time.

The Marquis de Montcalm was sent to New France to take command of the fight against the British. He had little respect for the *Canadiens* and the fighting style they had learned from their Native allies.

ARRIVAL OF MONTCALM

As General Vaudreuil prepared his soldiers to defeat the British in North America, tensions between Britain and France were rising in Europe. French forces had triumphed against Britain during the first two years of the Seven Years' War, which began in 1756. France's king, Louis XV, wanted a major victory in North America and believed that he needed a trained general from Europe to guarantee it. While the king thought that Vaudreuil had done a good job as governor, he did not think Vaudreuil was the best military leader. He sent a letter to Vaudreuil announcing that the Marquis de Montcalm, a promising young general, was on his way.

From the beginning, Governor Vaudreuil and General Montcalm did not get along. Montcalm thought the *Canadien* militia was undisciplined and poorly trained. He did not understand the Native style of warfare. For Montcalm, winning battles meant organized armies wearing bright uniforms and fighting in columns. Governor Vaudreuil resented the French general's attitude. He knew from earlier successes that *la petite guerre* style of fighting worked. Friction between the two men weakened New France just when it most needed strength.

In the spring of 1756, the French raided Fort Oswego. The British had built the fort as a base on a Native trade route in order to foster alliances with the First Nations people. The next year, Montcalm's forces captured Fort William Henry on the Richelieu River. Soon, the British colonies were calling for the destruction of New France.

To attack Quebec, James Wolfe sailed to Canada with a fleet of 186 ships and small boats, a full quarter of the British navy.

THE BRITISH PLAN

In 1758, the tide turned in favour of the British. With help from a new prime minister, William Pitt, the British decided to send thousands of fresh troops to overwhelm the French in North America. Soon after they arrived, the British launched their most ambitious campaign against Fort Duquesne, where the French were running short on supplies and ammunition. Unwilling to surrender the fort, the French burned it to the ground and retreated. The British then successfully attacked Fort Frontenac near Kingston. Now, nothing stood in the way of a British assault on Montreal and Quebec.

As the British soldiers closed in on the French forts from the west, the British naval fleet arrived from the east. On June 1, 1758, British ships prepared to attack the French fortress at Louisbourg, the gateway to the St. Lawrence River.

After weeks of bombardment, Louisbourg was surrendered to the British on July 26, 1758.

DEFEAT AT LOUISBOURG

Louisbourg was the key for Britain's conquest of New France. All French supply ships had to pass by the fort on their way to the St. Lawrence River and the fortress cities of Quebec and Montreal. The British planned to capture Fort Louisbourg, block supplies, corner French troops on a thin strip of land, and starve them into surrender. Two men, Jeffrey Amherst and James Wolfe, led the attack on Louisbourg. Augustin de Drucour, the governor of Louisbourg, knew he could not defeat the massive British forces, but he hoped to hold them off until the end of the summer.

For seven weeks in the summer of 1758, British cannons blasted the fort. The stone walls of Louisbourg began to crumble. Food and ammunition ran low. By mid-July, French forces at Louisbourg had lost the will to fight. Drucour surrendered on July 26. The British had cut the French supply lines to Canada. Without supplies and fresh troops, New France faced a grim fate. The British prepared to attack Quebec.

Telling Their Stories

MARIE-ANNE DE DRUCOUR

When the fortress of Louisbourg was attacked in the summer of 1758, its inhabitants fought to hold off the British a little longer. Among them was Marie-Anne de Drucour, the wife of the governor of Louisbourg. Watch *Canada: A People's History*, Episode 4, "Battle for a Continent: A Deterring and Dreadful Vengeance" (07:17:11 to 07:23:42). Find the nickname given to Mme Drucour and explain why you think it was appropriate. Write a paragraph to describe the steps you would have taken to save the fort if you had lived there at the time.

◄ Playback ►

1. Imagine you are Governor Vaudreuil of New France. Write a letter to the king of France explaining why you feel the tensions between the French and English in North America are reaching a boiling point.

2. Why were the French victorious at Fort Duquesne?

3. Why was it necessary for the French to stop the British from capturing the fort at Louisbourg?

4. How do you feel about the deportation of the Acadians?

5. Look at the picture on page 13 of the Acadians being expelled from their homes. With a partner, create a short dialogue between a British soldier and an Acadian refugee whom he is deporting.

The Back Story

Defending North America was a big responsibility for General Montcalm. The stakes were high, and he was far from home. He needed good advice about how to defend the French colonies in North America.

The Goal

Working in small groups, prepare a detailed memo to Montcalm describing a plan for victory.

The Steps

1. Analyse the strengths and weaknesses of the French and British colonies in 1755. Review this chapter or visit the school library for information. You can use a chart to organize your findings.
2. Offer ideas that might help Montcalm defend his colony against the larger English colonies. Listen to others' suggestions.
3. Create a plan for Montcalm to follow, including specific things he should and should not do.
4. Write your plan as a "Memo to Montcalm."
5. Attend a joint meeting of Montcalm's advisors (the rest of the class) and present your suggestions. Be prepared to answer questions or respond to comments from the other groups.

Evaluating Your Work

Think about these criteria as you complete your work. Your work should:
- include ideas that make sense
- show that your points support your overall idea
- show reasonable understanding of the military strategy of the time
- show a strong understanding of the events that were affecting New France
- be well organized and clearly written
- prepare you for discussion with others in your group or class.

History in Action   Biography of the Past

Montcalm

CHAPTER 2

CONQUEST OF NEW FRANCE

C.W. JEFFERYS

After the fall of Louisbourg, General Wolfe headed for Quebec with almost 200 ships and 15 000 men. The invasion force was so large it outnumbered the population of the city. Even worse for Quebec, Wolfe joined forces with British troops already stationed in North America. In all, Wolfe commanded 27 000 troops.

The French defeat at Louisbourg left the people of New France in terrible circumstances. With the main shipping route blocked, the winter of 1758 was one of famine and misery. Inside the walls of Quebec, the people slaughtered their horses for meat and rationed their bread until it finally ran out. Smallpox and typhus swept through the community. As they struggled to survive the winter, the *Canadiens* had to brace themselves for another British attack.

INSIDE THE WALLS OF QUEBEC

As the winter snow melted, so did the *Canadiens'* hopes. Farm families abandoned their land to find safety behind the stone walls of Quebec. In no time, the city was crowded with refugees. They tried to find shelter wherever they could—in churches, shops, barns, and seminaries. Those who couldn't find shelter were forced to live on the streets.

Many *Canadiens* wondered whether France was serious about protecting the colony. The king had sent only 400 new soldiers as reinforcements, not 4000 as Montcalm had requested. They were even more disheartened when they saw the sad state of the new troops. Thirty men deserted before their ship even reached Quebec. More than 40 arrived sick or dying from fever. The rest were loud, rude, rowdy, and frequently drunk. Montcalm had hoped for France's best soldiers. Instead, he got France's worst.

Quebec City, the capital of New France, before its capture by the British in 1759

The *Canadiens* also wondered whether France would send enough supplies. Merchants in the city were taking advantage of shortages by charging high prices for their goods. When the supply ships finally arrived from France in May 1759, they carried only one-third of what the people had requested. The *Canadiens'* worst fears were coming true—they were on their own.

Telling Their Stories

MARIE DE LA VISITATION

It was the job of the priests and nuns in the city of Quebec, such as Abbé Jean-Felix Richer and Mother Marie de la Visitation, to help the people in need. When the attack on Quebec came, Mother Marie de la Visitation noted the number of people staying in the convent: "Since our house was beyond the range of the enemy artillery, the poor people of the town didn't hesitate to seek refuge here. All the outbuildings were filled. The servant's quarters, the stable, the barn, even the attics were full." Watch *Canada: A People's History*, Episode 4, "Battle for a Continent: The River on Fire" (07:32:09 to 07:39:21). In role as a person living in Quebec City at the time, write and perform a dramatic monologue describing your life inside the walls of Quebec, before and during an attack.

General James Wolfe

Born into a military family, General James Wolfe joined the army at age 14. He served in battles in Scotland and Europe and quickly moved up the ranks.

James Wolfe was not a typical general. He was skinny and pale and suffered from seasickness, **rheumatism**, **tuberculosis**, and bladder infections. He often lay sick in bed for days. None of his weaknesses bothered Wolfe's men. They admired the risks he took when leading them in battle. They appreciated his refusal to whip soldiers as punishment and were relieved when he did away with the constant drills and boring exercises designed to ensure obedience. Older officers, however, were angry at Wolfe's new stature when he became major general after the fall of Louisbourg in 1758.

Wolfe was wounded three times in the final attack on the Plains of Abraham. Even as he lay dying, he called out orders to his troops. After his death, General Wolfe was recognized as a great hero of the British empire.

THE BRITISH ARE COMING

After his victory at Fort Louisbourg, General Wolfe was a hero when he returned to Britain. King George was so impressed that he promoted Wolfe to major general and asked him to return to New France, this time to lead the attack against Quebec. Quebec City was the largest and most important fortress in New France. It was the centre of trade, government, and the military. If Quebec could be conquered, the rest of the colony would fall.

In June 1759, General Wolfe sailed down the St. Lawrence River with a fleet of almost 200 ships. They landed at Ile d'Orléans, just south of the city of Quebec. According to Wolfe's scouts, a combined force of 16 000 French soldiers, Native warriors, and *Canadien* militia were waiting for them.

General James Wolfe

FRENCH FIRESHIPS

Even though he had a smaller army, Montcalm was in the stronger position. His men, stationed on hilltops, could see the invading forces from a distance. Wolfe's troops could only attack the fort by climbing the steep cliffs that rose from the riverbank, not knowing what awaited them at the top.

Before the British had a chance to work out a plan of attack, Montcalm launched a surprise assault. On June 28, 1759, in the middle of the night, the French forces set adrift 80 ships and rafts loaded with explosives. A soldier on each boat was to row as close as possible to the British ships. On a signal, he would ignite the gunpowder, jump into the water, and swim to shore. The plan backfired when one man ignited his cargo too early, well away from its target. Seeing the explosion, the rest of the men set their boats on fire. All 80 ships burned to ash without touching the British navy.

Near Quebec, Montcalm set adrift 80 boats loaded with gunpowder. When ignited, the fireships would destroy the British fleet. The plan failed when Montcalm's men ignited their cargoes too early.

A SOLDIER'S LIFE

When a young man signed up for military service, he was expected to buy his own musket, uniform, boots, blankets, and backpack. Since most men had to borrow money to buy their equipment, they began their military careers deeply in debt. The minimum length of service was seven years, but a soldier could have his debt paid if he agreed to stay longer. Some men stayed as long as 21 years. What was in it for the soldiers? Most young recruits were unemployed men from London, Ireland, and Scotland. Joining the military was the only way for them to avoid starvation and life on the streets.

British Half-Pay Pensioners

Soldiers who stayed in the military for 21 years were entitled to a pension—half their yearly pay for life. Many half-pay pensioners chose to stay in Canada, where they received small plots of land for free if they promised to serve in the local volunteer militia. Most were still young enough to marry, start families, and farm. Today, thousands of Canadians can trace their roots back to the half-pay pensioners.

A Soldier's Grin

For a young man to become a "lobster back," the slang name

for a soldier, he had to undergo a full medical inspection. The dental examination was the most important part. At a time when most young people lost their teeth, a soldier needed at least two opposing teeth—one tooth on top and one tooth directly below —so he could tear open the paper cartridge that carried his bullet and ammunition. A toothless man could not join the army.

Sideburns

During drills and battles, soldiers fired their guns while standing side by side in neat lines. The flintlocks, which made the muskets fire, threw out hot sparks. French and British soldiers grew sideburns to shield their faces from the flying sparks from guns that were firing beside them.

A Soldier's Dress

British and French soldiers usually wore their finest dress uniforms to battle. Tall hats and brilliantly coloured uniforms made soldiers look taller. Having all of the men execute their battle commands at the same time showed off their excellent training and was meant to impress and frighten the enemy.

Good Night, Gentlemen

Soldiers were often locked in their barracks at night to keep them from deserting. They slept under grey wool blankets on beds made of mattresses filled with straw. A good night's sleep was often ruined by the sound of the other 30 men snoring—or by bed bugs.

Women in the Barracks

Many soldiers who enlisted in the British army were married, but were usually separated from their wives and families for most of their 21 years of service. Each year, the British government held a lottery to allow up to 6 of every 100 soldiers to bring their wives with them. Married couples did not have their own rooms. The women had to sleep in the barracks with the other soldiers. A blanket pinned over the bunk was the only privacy the couples had.

From the Sources

VOICES FROM THE BATTLEFIELD

"The gunfire and bombardment terrorized the whole town. The women with their children, in great numbers near the Citadel, were continually in tears, wailing and praying. They huddled together and said the rosary."

"At noon, a bomb fell on widow Morand's house, set it on fire, and burned it to the ground, as well as widow Cheneverd's house, Mr. Cardenas's house, Mr. Dassier's house, and Madame Boishebert's house."

—Abbé Jean-Felix Richer

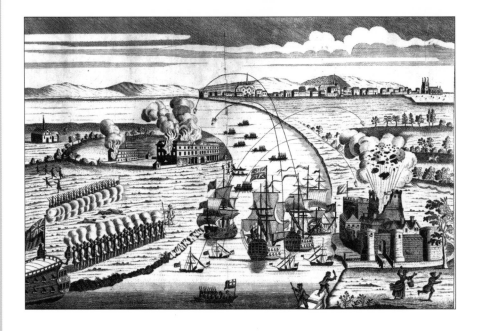

SIEGE OF QUEBEC

In July 1759, Wolfe landed 3000 soldiers at Pointe-Lévis, just across the river from Quebec. Now the walled city was within range of British cannon fire. The British bombarded the city. The *Canadiens* were terrified as hundreds of homes caught fire and buildings collapsed into rubble.

The **siege** of Quebec dragged on for the rest of the summer. When Wolfe ordered his troops to attack the cliffs, the French forces shot from above, killing hundreds of redcoats. The British suffered a terrible defeat. Wolfe came down with a fever and was bedridden for two weeks. Alarmed that winter was coming and their ships would get trapped in ice, Wolfe's officers organized an attack on Quebec from a spot 50 kilometres upriver. When heavy rain forced them to wait, Wolfe used the delay to tour the river in search of a new landing site. He chose a steep, rocky cliff a few kilometres from Quebec. His officers were shocked. Their men would have to spend hours scaling the cliff, not knowing what to expect at the top.

◀ Playback ▶

1. **What were the conditions in Quebec as the *Canadiens* prepared for the British attack?**

2. **Did Wolfe have the qualities of an effective leader?**

3. **Imagine you are an 11-year-old *Canadien* when Quebec is under siege. Describe your experience.**

4. **What do you think Montcalm should have done to defend Quebec?**

The battle of the Plains of Abraham, on September 13, 1759, lasted only 15 minutes, but it ended French control of North America.

THE PLAINS OF ABRAHAM

Wolfe's men landed at the site he had chosen. Under cover of night, they struggled up the side of the steep cliff, following a narrow goat path. Six hours later, at 5:00 in the morning, they reached the top and assembled in an abandoned field that had once belonged to Abraham Martin.

The French were caught completely by surprise. Their **sentries** were asleep, and Montcalm and his forces were stationed a few kilometres away. As soon as Montcalm heard about the British landing, he marched his troops to the field where Wolfe was waiting.

Wolfe was sure he would quickly defeat the poorly trained French. He knew, too, that he had no time to waste. His soldiers were exhausted after climbing all night. They had just enough food for one day and no tents or blankets. They had dragged two cannons up the cliff face, but had brought the wrong ammunition for one.

After his death, Wolfe's body was returned to Britain where he was honoured with a state funeral. He was buried in Westminster Abbey among the great heroes of the empire.

Battle Lines

Wolfe's men arranged themselves in two lines stretching from the cliff to the woods two kilometres away. Montcalm assembled his army of French soldiers, *Canadien* militia, and Native warriors in three columns on the hillside, ready to charge and smash the British lines. But his troops were disorganized and couldn't keep their columns together. They fired too early and missed their targets.

As the French forces advanced, Wolfe gave the most important command of his life. He ordered his men to load their muskets with two bullets rather than one, so that they could fire twice as many shots at the enemy. When the French forces were just 40 metres away, the British commanders gave the order to fire. A roaring **volley** of bullets ripped through the ragged French line. When the second line fired, the French turned and broke ranks. Behind them charged the Fraser

Highlanders, ferocious hand-to-hand fighters from Scotland known for their skill with swords. The French ran for their lives. The battle had lasted just 15 minutes.

Both Wolfe and Montcalm were wounded. Wolfe died on the battlefield. Montcalm died the next day in the hospital. His body was buried under the floor of the Ursuline nuns' chapel in a crater made by a British cannon ball.

The Last Stand

After the French defeat at the Plains of Abraham, the citizens of Quebec learned that their defenders were abandoning the city without a fight. Men and women jeered and pelted soldiers with whatever they could find. On September 18, 1759, the British flag was raised for the first time in Canada, at the top of Mountain Street, inside the walls of Quebec.

Quebec was in ruins. Most buildings were destroyed, and people were hungry. Farmers had abandoned their land when British troops appeared in their villages, and their crops rotted in the fields. Unwilling to live under British rule, many *seigneurs* returned to France.

The British had 3000 troops in the city. That fall and winter the British and French faced famine together. Soldiers were ordered to share their rations, to shelter with their enemies, and to work together to rebuild the city.

After another harsh winter, both sides waited to see whether Britain or France would be the first to send fresh troops and supplies. The new British commander, James Murray, waited in Quebec. The new French general, François-Gaston de Lévis, waited in Montreal, the last undefeated French post. When the first supply ships finally pulled into port in the spring, they were waving British flags. General Lévis understood that all was lost. Without food or ammunition, he voluntarily surrendered. New France had fallen.

This is a watercolour of a French Marine soldier in uniform serving on board the warships at Rochefort, France, circa 1718.

Propaganda in Art: Death Portraits

Great emotion followed the deaths of Wolfe and Montcalm. Their deaths were commemorated in paintings that portrayed them as great heroes of epic battles. Look closely at the pictures, though, and you will notice some details that don't make sense.

Death of Wolfe

The Death of Wolfe by Benjamin West was painted 11 years after Wolfe died. Although powerful, the painting does not accurately depict what really happened. For example, a Native man is leaning thoughtfully at Wolfe's feet, but no Native people fought on the British side—they were allied with the French. The man's presence is also ironic, because Wolfe had little respect for First Nations people.

There is a large group of soldiers and officers gathered around the dying general, but so many officers would probably not stop fighting in the middle of a battle. This painting, however, is the most popular and dramatic of many portraits of Wolfe's death. To the British, it represents bravery, courage, and nobility.

Death of Montcalm

The Death of Montcalm is also full of mistakes. The most obvious is that Montcalm did not die on the battlefield; he died the next day in a hospital bed. There is a palm tree in the background, but palm trees are tropical plants that grow in warm regions, not in the northern climate of Quebec. The Native warriors in the foreground look like the people of South America, not like members of the First Nations in North America. The most interesting fiction is the figure of Wolfe in the background, dying like a common soldier.

Which painting do you prefer? Which painting best portrays courage and heroism? What do the mistakes in these paintings tell you about historical images?

◄ Playback ►

1. Why did the British find it difficult to capture Quebec?

2. What problems did Wolfe face as leader of the British forces?

3. Why was Wolfe victorious at the Plains of Abraham?

4. How do you think the *Canadiens* felt when they realized that the British had conquered New France?

The Back Story

The battle of the Plains of Abraham is one of the best-know pieces of Canada's history. We know the dates, we know about the short battle, and we know the names of the British and French generals. We can also learn by investigating and imagining human reactions, observations, thoughts, and feelings.

The Goal

Role-play one of the following people being interviewed by a journalist outside the walls of Quebec on the day the city is attacked. Assume you are speaking directly from the battlefield. You can be a French or British officer, a *Canadien* militiaman, a wounded French, British, or Native fighter, Montcalm, or Wolfe. You can also choose to be the wife or child of a *habitant* fighter watching the battle from inside the walls of the city.

The Steps

1. Decide which character you will role play.
2. Choose an appropriate name.
3. Research more about the battle of Quebec by reading this chapter, viewing Episode 4 of *Canada: A People's History*, using online or library resources, viewing images that convey the sights, sounds, and emotions of the battle, and so on.
4. Write a simple outline of what you think your character would say if he or she had one minute to speak to a journalist.
5. Practise your script to make sure you know it.
6. When the class is organized on the field of battle, present your script when your name is called. Remain quiet while the other characters speak.
7. After you have heard from everyone, discuss the scripts.

History in Action

Live from the Plains of Abraham

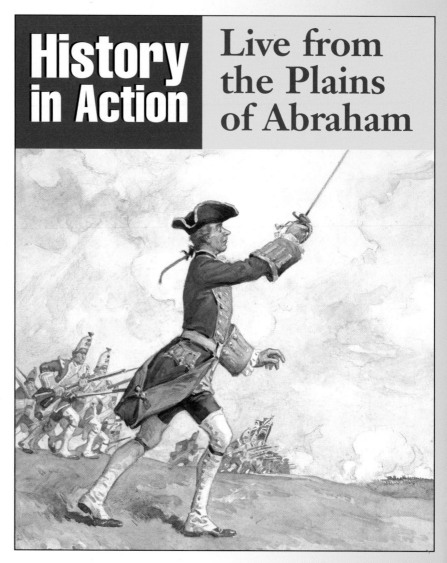

Evaluating Your Work

Think about these criteria as you complete your work. Your work should:
- be carefully researched
- be based on historical events
- reflect a knowledge of the conventions of a news report
- be carefully rehearsed and clearly presented
- include an opportunity for you to listen carefully as others report from the battlefield.

CHAPTER 3

BUILDING A NEW CONTINENT

Pierre de Rigaud de Vaudreuil de Cavagnial, governor of New France

After their loss on the Plains of Abraham, the people of New France knew the fight was over. France was not going to send reinforcements to continue the battle. It was too busy fighting with the British in Europe.

The Marquis de Vaudreuil had no choice but to arrange the conditions of Quebec's surrender. He was able to win three important guarantees for the *Canadiens*: the right to speak the French language, the right to keep their land, and the right to practise their Catholic faith. These were significant guarantees —in the rest of the British empire, Catholics did not have many rights. The terms of surrender were completed on September 8, 1760. King George II of Britain now controlled most of North America.

The Bishop's House in Quebec City, surrounded by the ruins of war

GOING HOME

Under the terms of surrender, the *Canadien* militia was forced to disband. The men returned to their homes and farms, grateful to be alive. Many *seigneurs* returned to France. French soldiers also returned home, except for about 500 who stayed behind to live with their new *Canadien* wives. The British left a small force of 3000 men to maintain law and order and sent the rest of their soldiers to other posts in North America.

PICKING UP THE PIECES

When the British flag was raised for the first time in Quebec on September 18, 1759, the British discovered that there was little left to claim or steal. The British bombardment had almost completely destroyed the city. There was little food, and wood for building and heat was scarce. As winter set in, British soldiers learned that their uniforms were useless in the harsh Canadian temperatures. Many died from frostbite, pneumonia, and scurvy. The British eventually learned the Native remedies for scurvy—drinking cedar tea and chewing pine needles.

Telling Their Stories

BENJAMIN FRANKLIN

Benjamin Franklin was an important leader in the Thirteen Colonies. He hated the French and had a dream of an English and Protestant country ruled by the British.

Before the **conquest** of New France, Franklin's newspaper, The *Pennsylvania Gazette*, was filled with articles about his vision. Watch *Canada: A People's History*, Episode 4, "Battle for a Continent: Dangerous Vision" (07:05:31 to 07:10:01). Listen to all of the statements that Franklin makes. How would you describe his views about the French and the First Nations? How do you think his views would make him act?

After the conquest, Franklin said: "No one can rejoice more sincerely than I do on the Reduction of Canada. If we keep [Canada], all the country, from the St. Lawrence to Mississippi, will in another century be filled with British people." Write an editorial, in role as Franklin, to be published in his newspaper following Britain's conquest of New France.

British Hopes

Benjamin Franklin was one of the British colonists who predicted that the people of Quebec would become British after the conquest of New France. He wrote: "Many will choose to remove if they can be allowed to sell their lands, improvements and effects: the rest, in that thin-settled country, will in less than half a century … be blended and incorporated with our people in both language and manners."

THE TREATY OF PARIS, 1763

The vicious Seven Years' War between Britain and France, which had begun in 1756 and was fought in both Europe and North America, was finally over. Britain had won at an enormous cost in both money and men.

In 1761, the British and French met in Paris to negotiate the terms of a peace treaty, called the Treaty of Paris. William Pitt represented Britain. The Duke of Choiseul represented France. No one spoke for the First Nations. William Pitt and the Duke of Choiseul were both skilled negotiators, but they despised one another. Because of their differences, the treaty talks dragged on for two years.

Britain offered France the choice of keeping either Canada or the tiny, sugar-rich Caribbean island of Guadeloupe. France chose Guadeloupe, knowing there was more money to be made from sugar than from furs. It also kept the tiny islands of St. Pierre and Miquelon in the Gulf of St. Lawrence so it could continue to fish the rich waters of the Atlantic coast. The two islands still belong to France today. The British would have control of the Ohio River valley, with land reserved for First Nations and for the fur trade.

On September 8, 1760, Governor Vaudreuil of Quebec surrendered Montreal to the commander of the British forces, Jeffrey Amherst.

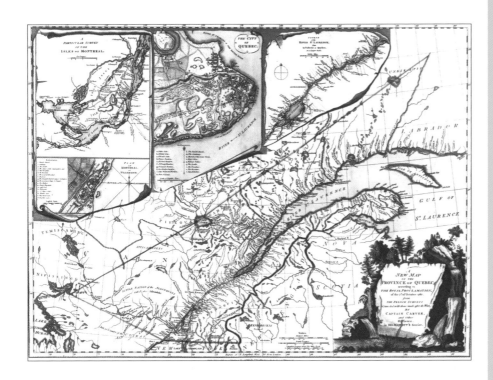

The boundaries of the
Province of Quebec as
defined by the
Proclamation Act of 1763

Finally, in 1763, Britain and France signed the treaty, a document that would change North America forever.

QUEBEC: A NEW BRITISH COLONY

The British now governed 65 000 French Catholics. They had predicted that most of the French colonists would return to France. Those who stayed, they believed, would eventually learn English, become Protestant, and adopt British culture. They were wrong. The privileged French upper class had already left. Those who remained were *Canadiens*. They had no desire to abandon the land of their ancestors. To the *Canadiens*, Canada—not France—was home.

◀ Playback ▶

1. **What did Vaudreuil win for the conquered *Canadiens* after the battle of Quebec? In your view, which guarantee was most important? Why?**

2. **Who returned to France? Who stayed behind in the new British colony?**

3. **Create a graphic organizer to help identify the advantages and disadvantages of the Treaty of Paris for France.**

4. **If you were *Canadien* in 1759, how would you view your future? Be specific.**

Chief Pontiac in council with the elders of his Ottawa First Nation

THE FIRST NATIONS AND BRITISH RULE

The First Nations had to face the fact that their French allies were gone. For over a century, the French and First Nations people had forged strong connections through marriages, trading, and gift giving. Now, everything had changed. The British saw no reason to continue the French practice of gift-giving ceremonies or to respect Native rights.

Chief Pontiac missed the French more than most Native leaders. An Ottawa chief from the Ohio valley, he had declared himself a son of the king of France. During the 1750s, Pontiac and his warriors fought as French allies to keep English settlers away from Native land. To Pontiac, the end of the gift-giving ritual was a great insult. He called on the Ottawa nation to push the British out of the region. Pontiac's strategy was simple—drive the British from the northwest and await the return of French rule.

NEL

Attacking British Forts

In the spring of 1763, the Ottawa nation, along with warriors from the Huron, Delaware, Miami, Seneca, Shawnee, Kickapoo, and Chippewa nations, launched a series of attacks on British forts. To send a threatening message to the British, Pontiac's warriors scalped their prisoners of war.

An attack at Fort Detroit turned out to be the beginning of a long siege. As it wore on, conditions became more difficult for Pontiac and his people. Food and water ran low. Some of Pontiac's own warriors started to abandon the fight to take up the seasonal hunt.

One Native group caught smallpox. The source of the disease was the British general, Jeffrey Amherst, who had decided to use germ warfare to conquer Pontiac's people. He had his men cut blankets infected with small-pox into small pieces. They placed the pieces in tin boxes, which they gave to the Native warriors as gifts of medicine. When the boxes were opened, smallpox spread rapidly and thousands of Native people died.

General Jeffrey Amherst

The next blow came in October 1763. The king of France informed Pontiac that he would not send soldiers to drive out the British. Pontiac was devastated. He tried to rebuild his forces and carry on the fight, but finally, in 1764, exhausted and defeated, he quit. A few years later, he was killed by an Illinois warrior named Black Dog. His murder was thought to be part of a British plot.

From the Sources

At Fort Michilimackinac, located on the southern shore that connected Lake Huron and Lake Michigan, the Ojibwa chief Minavavana warned a group of English traders:

"Englishman, although you have conquered the French you have not yet conquered us! We are not your slaves. These lakes, these woods, and mountains, were left us by our ancestors. They are our inheritance and we will part with them to none ... Englishman, our Father, the king of France, employed our young men to make war upon your nation. In his warfare, many of them have been killed and it is our custom to retaliate, until such time as the spirits of the slain are satisfied.

But the spirits of the slain are to be satisfied in either of two ways. The first is the spilling of the blood of the nation by which they fell, the other, by covering the bodies of the dead, and thus allaying the resentment of their relations. This is done by making presents. Englishman, your king has not sent us any presents, nor entered into any treaty with us, therefore he and we are still at war."

Les Canadiens

"Little, very little, will content the New Subjects [*Canadiens*], but nothing will satisfy the Licentious Fanatics Trading here, but the expulsion of the Canadians who are perhaps the bravest and the best race upon the Globe, a Race, who could they be **indulged** with a few privileges which laws of England deny Roman Catholics at home, would soon get the better of every national **antipathy** to the Conquerors and become the most faithful and most useful set of men in the American Empire."

—Governor James Murray

General James Murray, first British governor of Canada

A NEW FRIENDSHIP

The task of rebuilding Quebec fell to James Murray, the new governor of the colony. He also had to rebuild *Canadien* morale. His leadership was soon tested by the arrival of British merchants from the Thirteen Colonies who were anxious to cash in on new business opportunities. Murray respected and liked the *Canadiens*, but did not feel the same about the British newcomers. The merchants, Murray told a friend in a letter, were "in general the most immoral collection of men I ever knew." They would soon become serious troublemakers.

THE PROCLAMATION ACT

In 1763, the British government introduced the Proclamation Act. It called for an appointed military governor to oversee the colony and an elected **assembly** of English Protestants. It also imposed British laws and courts. The Act returned some land in the Ohio River valley to the First Nations and forbade British settlers from taking over Native hunting grounds. Finally, the Act protected the right of the Catholic *Canadiens* to practise their religion.

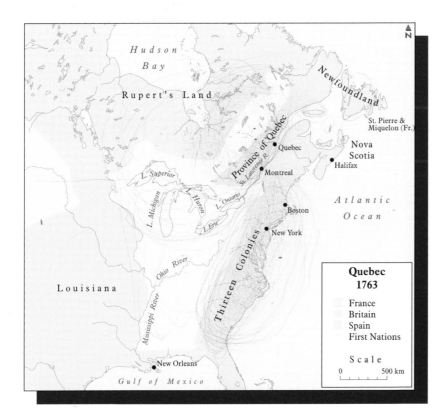

Quebec 1763
- France
- Britain
- Spain
- First Nations

Scale
0   500 km

Thomas Walker and the Merchants

Some British merchants thought that the Proclamation Act was too generous. Nowhere else in the British empire did Catholics have the right to practise their religion. The merchants demanded that business be conducted in English only and insisted that Murray enforce the law forbidding Catholics from holding office. If Murray agreed, a handful of British merchants would dominate 65 000 French Canadians.

The merchants' leader was an aggressive man named Thomas Walker. An angry Walker sailed to Britain to deliver a petition demanding that Murray be removed from office and that Catholics lose their privileges. The petition was half successful. Murray was removed from office. His replacement, Guy Carleton, had no better luck satisfying Walker and his supporters.

The Proclamation Act, 1763

The following are the terms of the Proclamation Act:

- The colony is subject to British criminal and civil law.

- The colony must establish an elected assembly.

- Only British subjects can hold public office.

- Territories west of the Appalachian mountains are reserved for the First Nations.

- The seigneurial system is abolished.

- English is the colony's official language.

- Catholics may practise their faith, but the Catholic Church no longer has a say in government decisions.

◄ Playback ►

1. **Why did the Native leaders not trust the British? Why did they decide to go to war under Pontiac? What was the result of Chief Pontiac's rebellion?**

2. **How did Governor Murray view his new *Canadien* subjects? Why?**

3. **Would you agree with the boundary changes in the Proclamation Act if you were (a) a French Canadian; (b) a member of a First Nation; (c) a British colonist?**

The Back Story

After the British conquest of New France, newspapers were quickly established in Quebec. The view of life they represented depended on whether they were printed by French or English publishers.

The Goal

Create a newspaper that reports on the conquest of New France. Each newspaper will include a title; at least three articles that include the views of a French colonist, an English colonist, and a Native person; at least one editorial; at least one editorial cartoon; and at least six classified ads.

The Steps

1. Decide as a group whether your newspaper will support the French or the English.
2. Select an appropriate title for your newspaper.
3. Research the politics, economy, and lifestyle of the people of New France after the conquest. Find information in the school or public library and on the Internet.
4. Work closely with other team members. You can choose one person as editor to keep everyone on track.
5. Produce your newspaper by writing and peer-editing stories, creating or finding relevant art, and designing an eye-catching and easy-to-read layout.
6. Present your complete newspaper to your class and post on the bulletin board.

Evaluating Your Work

Think about these criteria as you complete your work. Your work should:
- be based on historical events
- be thoroughly researched
- clearly support your point of view
- represent thoughts and opinions clearly
- demonstrate an understanding of some conventions of newspaper writing and layout
- be neat and well presented.

History in Action   Creating a Newspaper

A colonial newspaper

CHAPTER 4

QUEBEC AND THE AMERICAN REVOLUTION

Montreal, 1762

Governor Murray was gone, but the British merchants were not happy when Guy Carleton was appointed as the new governor of Quebec in 1768. They had hoped that James Murray's replacement would side with them and end the religious privileges of the *Canadiens*. But Guy Carleton believed in protecting *Canadien* rights, which led to the creation of the Quebec Act in 1774. The Act turned out to be one of the causes of the American Revolution in the Thirteen Colonies.

Guy Carleton had joined the British army at the age of 14. By 1768, when he was appointed governor of Quebec, he was a highly decorated general. He had served as an officer during the Seven Years' War in Europe and had been wounded at the battle of the Plains of Abraham. He served two terms as governor of Quebec (1768–1778 and 1785–1795). Carleton died in 1808.

GOVERNOR GUY CARLETON

Guy Carleton was a thoughtful man. He understood that the *Canadiens* had a unique society and history. "This country," he wrote, "must to the end of time be peopled by the *Canadien* race, who have already taken such firm root, and got to so great a height, that any new stock transplanted will be totally hid and imperceptible amongst them, except in the towns of Quebec and Montreal."

Carleton believed that by granting language, religious, and legal rights to the *Canadiens*, they would become loyal subjects of the British crown. He allowed leading French *Canadiens* to hold 12 seats on the 20-member governing council. Nine of the new French council members had won the Croix de Saint-Louis, France's highest medal of honour, for fighting against the British during the Seven Years' War. By offering these war heroes a seat in government, Carleton earned the trust and loyalty of the *Canadien* community.

FEARS OF THE *CANADIENS*

Despite Governor Carleton's support, the *Canadiens* were still worried. They were afraid that under British law, their old legal contracts, marriage customs, and property deeds would change. Alarmed by the continuing demands of Thomas Walker and his fellow merchants, the *Canadiens* feared that they might someday lose their language, culture, religion, and land. They knew that the British had expelled the Acadians in 1755 for refusing to give up their Catholic faith. In England, Catholics did not have the right to work in government offices, to vote, or to serve on juries.

After so many generations in New France, and so much bloodshed, the *Canadiens* did not want to lose everything. Carleton understood their fears. He knew how much they valued their language and religion. He realized that replacing their traditional French civil law with British law would lead to chaos and confusion.

After Britain took over Quebec, life gradually settled down for *Canadien* farmers, especially for those whose French-speaking *seigneurs* remained. Many others had new English-speaking landlords, who were mostly British officers. They had purchased the estates of *seigneurs* who had decided to return to France. The new British landlords would play an important role in the former French colony.

◀ Playback ▶

1. **Why were English merchants unhappy with Governors Murray and Carleton?**

2. **What was Carleton's goal when dealing with *Canadien* rights? Do you agree or disagree with his point of view? Explain.**

3. **Outline the *Canadiens'* main fears as they faced a future as British subjects.**

Petition from the *Canadiens*

"… [G]rant us, in common with your other subjects, the rights and privileges of citizens of England. Then our fears will be removed, and we shall pass our lives in tranquility and happiness, and shall be always ready to sacrifice them for the glory of our prince and the good of our country."

Boston harbour

TROUBLE IN THE THIRTEEN COLONIES

During Carleton's first term as governor, from 1768 to 1778, trouble was brewing in the Thirteen Colonies. People there were growing increasingly frustrated with high British taxes, and they wanted more say in government decisions. Many dreamed of breaking away from Britain to become an independent country. The British merchants in Quebec sympathized with them.

Carleton realized that if a war of independence broke out in the Thirteen Colonies, he would not be able to count on help from the British merchants. Unless Britain won the loyalty of the *Canadien* majority once and for all, it risked losing its Canadian colony. In 1770, Carleton sailed to London, prepared to convince the British government to take care of the problems with the merchants in Quebec. With him he carried a **petition** from the *Canadiens*, promising their loyalty in return for guaranteed language, religious, and legal rights.

Building to Revolution

Britain needed money to support the colonies in its vast empire and to pay for its navy and troops. King George decided to place new taxes on the people of the Thirteen Colonies. In 1765, the British Parliament passed the Stamp Act, which forced the colonists to pay taxes in gold or silver for newspapers, playing cards, wills, and licenses.

Many colonists were outraged that they were being forced to pay taxes to Britain but had no political representation in the British Parliament, where all the decisions about the colonies were made. They demanded that Britain remove the stamp tax. Britain refused. Instead, it decided to place more new taxes on the colonies. Some merchants in the colonies started smuggling goods, including tea, to avoid paying taxes to Britain.

On December 16, 1773, a group of colonists dressed as Mohawk warriors dumped crates of tea in Boston harbour to protest Britain's Tea Act. Called the Boston Tea Party, it was one of the turning points in the Thirteen Colonies that led to the American Revolution.

In 1773, Britain passed the Tea Act, which allowed its British East India Company to sell tea directly to the colonists. It was the last straw for many merchants who had been selling smuggled tea in the colonies. On December 16, 1773, a group of men dressed as Mohawk warriors boarded three ships in Boston harbour. The ships belonged to the British East India Company and were loaded with tea. The men destroyed hundreds of crates of tea and threw them into the harbour.

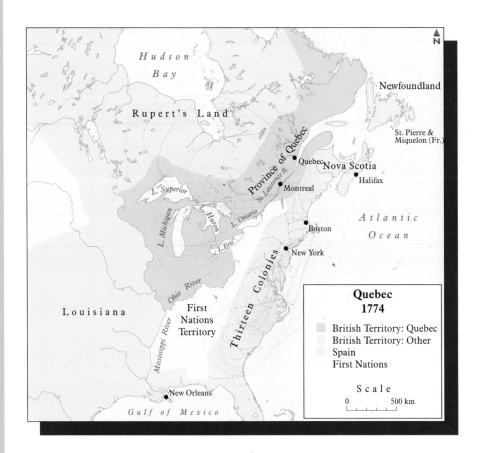

To prevent American colonists from taking over fur-trading lands and angering First Nations, the British Parliament handed the western lands back to the colony of Quebec in the Quebec Act of 1774.

THE QUEBEC ACT, 1774

When Governor Guy Carleton arrived in London, England in 1770 with the petition from the *Canadiens*, he found that the British government was far more concerned about problems in the Thirteen Colonies than about *Canadien* rights in Quebec. Carleton spent the next four years trying to convince British leaders to guarantee *Canadien* rights. Finally, in the spring of 1774, the British House of Commons passed the Quebec Act.

The Quebec Act strengthened the British empire by making Quebec both British and French. It guaranteed freedom of religion and allowed the *Canadiens* to hold public office, serve on juries, and vote in elections. It kept British criminal law, but returned the system of French civil law to the colony. It also extended Quebec's boundaries to include the rich fur-trading areas between the Ohio and Mississippi rivers.

The Act established a province made up of two cultures, English and French. For the *Canadiens*, the Quebec Act promised cultural survival. Instead of forcing the *Canadiens* to adopt British language, religion, and culture, the Act recognized that they were unique.

In the Thirteen Colonies

The leaders in the Thirteen Colonies were furious when they heard about the Quebec Act. They were angry that the Act extended the boundaries of Canada into the Ohio River valley, an area the colony of Virginia was trying to claim. They resented the offer of French language rights and freedom of religion for Catholics. To the people of the Thirteen Colonies, the Quebec Act was a slap in the face, further proof that King George would never listen to them. It was the last straw. They were ready to revolt.

From the Sources
AGAINST THE QUEBEC ACT

The Quebec Act was passed by the British Parliament on June 22, 1774. The vote was 56 in favour and 20 opposed. Most of the members of Parliament who voted for the Act wanted to ensure that Britain would have *Canadien* support if the Thirteen Colonies revolted. Those who voted against it opposed the special privileges that the Act gave Quebec and the *Canadiens*. In the Thirteen Colonies, the Quebec Act set tempers flaring.

"I should think it material not to give [the Canadiens*] directly their own law again; it keeps up that perpetual dependence upon their ancient laws and customs, which will ever make [them] a distinct people."*

—Lord Cavendish, British member of Parliament

"The finger of God points out a mighty Empire to our sons; the Savages of the wilderness were never expelled to make room in this, the best part of the continent, for idolaters and slaves."

—*New York Journal*

"It appears to me the greatest stake that was ever played for, no less than whether Americans, and their endless generations shall enjoy the common rights of mankind, or be worse than Eastern slaves; the trial must now come to issue as 'open war' is declared by the Boston Port Act ... and above all the Quebec Bill."

—Benjamin Franklin

Benjamin Franklin

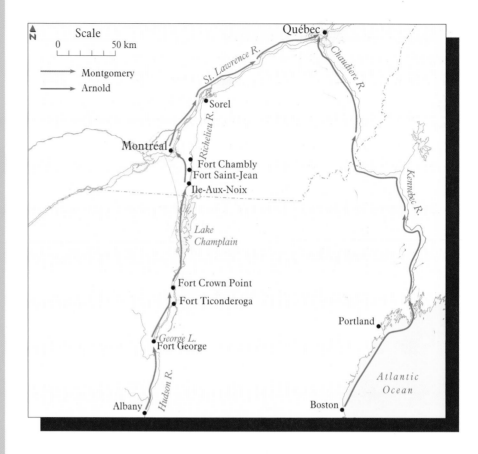

The American invasion routes of General Montgomery and General Arnold

AMERICAN INVASION OF CANADA

The conflict in the Thirteen Colonies finally exploded in 1775. Leaders in the colonies asked the *Canadiens* to join them in revolting against British rule, but they would not risk the rights granted to them in the Quebec Act. With war approaching, Governor Carleton was worried. What would the *Canadiens* do when they learned that France had sided with the American colonies against the British?

Taking Montreal

General George Washington and the American forces set out to weaken British forces by taking the fortress of Quebec, which provided a naval base and a supply line for British forces. In September 1775, Generals Richard Montgomery and Benedict Arnold led their armies into Quebec.

On November 13, Montgomery and his forces arrived at Montreal. They met little resistance because Governor Carleton had moved his soldiers to Quebec City. Montgomery quickly took the city and received a hero's welcome. Montreal was now in the hands of the American revolutionaries.

The Battle of Quebec City

General Benedict Arnold headed for Quebec City with his force of 1200 men. Deep in the Quebec wilderness, they got lost in a winter storm. Faced with starvation, the men were forced to eat their shoe leather, their cardboard cartridge boxes, and their dog. By the time he reached Quebec City in November 1775, Arnold had lost 500 soldiers to desertion and death.

After camping outside of the city for nearly two months, Arnold and Montgomery planned a surprise attack. The two generals and their armies would wear British uniforms, sneak into the city at night, and attack Governor Carleton and his forces. Montgomery would enter from one gate and Arnold from another, with the two armies meeting in the middle.

British forces arriving to attack Quebec in the spring of 1776. Why do you think they would attack in the spring rather than in the winter?

On December 30, during a heavy blizzard, Arnold and Montgomery launched two rockets to signal the start of the battle and moved their forces into the city. The British responded with a volley of musket fire. Montgomery was killed instantly, and many other soldiers were killed or fled in fear. On the other end of the city, Arnold marched his troops through the gate. Carleton and his men opened fire. Leading his troops deep into the city, General Arnold was wounded. With no one left to lead the American troops, they were quickly defeated.

THE AMERICAN RETREAT

With Benedict Arnold in hospital, General David Wooster was left in charge. He decided to wait out the winter before launching another attack. In the meantime, he turned his attention to the *Canadiens* in Montreal. Wooster banned church celebrations at Christmas and arrested leading citizens on charges of spying. When the Americans ran out of gold to buy food, they simply took it. The *Canadiens*, who had welcomed the Americans as heroes, now planned to rebel. In the spring, the American Congress sent Benjamin Franklin to negotiate with the *Canadiens* in Montreal. He arrived to find the *Canadiens* hungry and sick. After 12 days of talking, Franklin decided that the *Canadiens* would not join the American Revolution, so he returned home.

On May 6, 1776, British warships with 10 000 men arrived at Quebec. A month later, Arnold's troops retreated from Montreal, and the Americans gave up their hope of taking over Canada.

In July 1776, the Thirteen Colonies declared their independence from Britain, and the United States was born. War between the British and the Americans dragged on until 1783, when Britain finally withdrew its forces from the United States. British North America was changed forever. Governor Guy Carleton's vision for a Canada where English and French worked together would endure.

Benedict Arnold

Benedict Arnold, who became one of history's famous traitors, was a dedicated patriot when the American Revolution began.

In 1775, Arnold led the American forces that set out to take the fortress of Quebec. When they failed, Arnold returned to home with a musket ball lodged in his leg. Serving under General George Washington, Arnold battled the British again, and received another injury.

Arnold felt that he had sacrificed a great deal serving in the American forces, and was unhappy about how he was being treated. He demanded that the American Congress recognize his **seniority** in the army and give him a good pension.

Later, Arnold married Peggy Shippen, the daughter of a wealthy Loyalist judge. They lived an extravagant life, which Arnold's army salary could not support. He started using army wagons for personal trips, and sailing customers to England in an American trade ship. Both actions were serious offenses. Arnold was **court-martialled** and found guilty.

Arnold turned against the American government. In 1780, he sent a letter to British authorities, offering them an important American fort in New York, under his command, in exchange for a payment of 20 000 British pounds and a job as a

general in the British army. An American officer intercepted his letter, and Arnold barely escaped arrest. He spent the last year of the American Revolutionary War fighting for the British on American soil. At the end of the war in 1783, Arnold settled in Saint John, New Brunswick, and eventually retired to London, England. Despised and distrusted by the British and unwelcome in the United States, Arnold died broke and forgotten in 1801.

◄ Playback ►

1. **Why was it so important for Governor Carleton to win the loyalty of the *Canadiens*?**

2. **In your view, what were the most important terms of the Quebec Act?**

3. **Why was the Quebec Act so important to Canada in general and to French Canada in particular?**

4. **Why did the 1775 American invasion of Canada fail?**

5. **How would you explain the *Canadien* reaction to the American invasion? In your view, did their stand make sense?**

The Back Story

Since the English and French communities in Quebec disagreed about the future of the colony, they both tried to convince the British government to make the changes they desired.

The Goal

In role as a French or an English group, you will present a petition to the British king to help him decide what to do with the French colony in North America.

The Steps

1. With your group, prepare an oral presentation to deliver to the king and his advisors. Your petition must include:
   a) the location of the boundaries of Quebec
   b) a statement of the rights and privileges granted and/or denied to both the English and the French in Quebec and a justification for your decision
   c) the government structure you propose for Quebec
   d) the rules that will govern land ownership, agriculture, the fur trade, religion, and language.
2. Present your petition to the class.
3. Acting as the king and his advisors, the class will discuss all proposals and then make a final decision about the fate of the French colony.
4. Together, decide on each of the elements of the petitions as outlined in Step 1, and justify all decisions.
5. Discuss as a group the decision-making process. Are your results the same as the Quebec Act or are they different? Why?

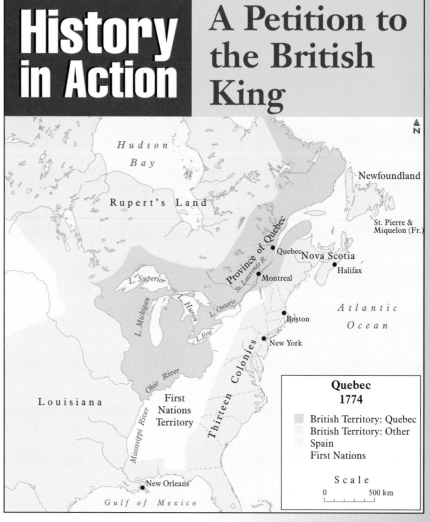

History in Action

A Petition to the British King

Map: **Quebec 1774**
- British Territory: Quebec
- British Territory: Other
- Spain
- First Nations

Scale
0   500 km

Evaluating Your Work

Think about these criteria as you complete your work. Your work should:
- be based on historical fact
- clearly defend your group's point of view
- follow all the guidelines described above
- include both a written and an oral component
- be well written, using proper grammar and spelling
- be of the required length.

CHAPTER 5

FAST FORWARD

The story of the conquest of New France did not end with the French defeat on the Plains of Abraham in 1759. Nor did it end with the Quebec Act in 1774, when *Canadiens* in the British colony of Quebec were assured of their rights to practise their Catholic faith, speak French, vote and hold office, and follow French civil law. The *Canadiens'* fears of being overwhelmed by English-speaking Protestants continued to haunt Canadian history, and many issues that loomed large more than 200 years ago still play an important role in the lives of Canadians today.

One of Canada's biggest political rallies occurred on October 27, 1995, just before Quebec's second referendum on separation. Thousands of Canadians from across the country travelled to Montreal to show support for Quebec remaining in Canada.

TIMELINE

1791 Constitution Act divides Quebec into Upper and Lower Canada

1841 Province of Canada formed from union of Upper and Lower Canada

1867 Confederation

1885 Northwest Rebellion

1837 Rebellions in Upper and Lower Canada

1869 Red River Rebellion

1914 First World War begins

CONSTITUTION ACT, 1791

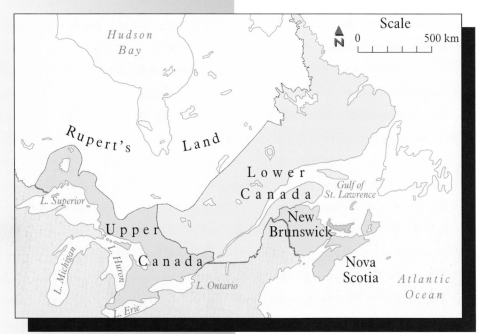

The Constitution Act of 1791 divided the old colony of Quebec into Upper and Lower Canada. In 1841, following Lord Durham's Report, Lower Canada was renamed Canada East and Upper Canada was renamed Canada West in the new Province of Canada.

After the Quebec Act in 1774, the next major change in the lives of the *Canadiens* came at the end of the American Revolutionary War in 1783, when thousands of British **Loyalists** from the United States arrived in Quebec. Most settled in the western part of the colony, on the shores of Lake Ontario and Lake Erie, in present-day Ontario. Before long, they were calling for a British form of government in the colony of Quebec.

Once again, English-speaking strangers were raising *Canadiens'* fears about the survival of their way of life. Britain's solution to the new French-English tensions in Quebec was the Constitution Act of 1791. It divided Quebec into two provinces. The eastern part became Lower Canada, the home of the *Canadiens*, where government business would be conducted in both French and English. The western part became Upper Canada, home to British settlers, where government business would be conducted only in English.

TIMELINE

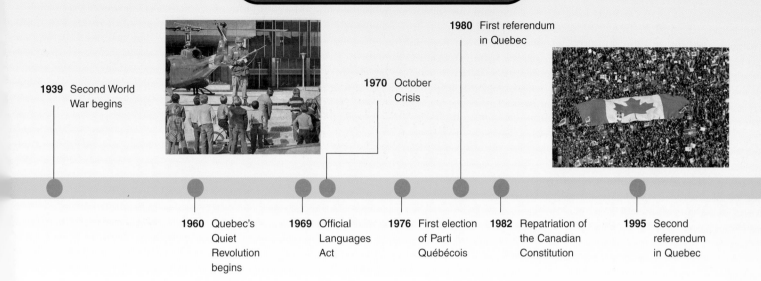

1939 Second World War begins

1960 Quebec's Quiet Revolution begins

1969 Official Languages Act

1970 October Crisis

1976 First election of Parti Québécois

1980 First referendum in Quebec

1982 Repatriation of the Canadian Constitution

1995 Second referendum in Quebec

REBELLION, 1837

By 1837, some *Canadiens* in Lower Canada were determined to reverse the results of the conquest, and took up arms against British rule. They fought British troops in three battles, where many men were killed and injured. In the end, the British governor and his army defeated the rebels.

The new governor, Lord Durham, proposed two steps to put an end to the trouble in Canada. First, he recommended that elected representatives, rather than officials appointed by Britain, make all the important local decisions in Upper and Lower Canada. Second, he urged the British government to unite the two colonies and flood Lower Canada with English-speaking immigrants. Lord Durham hoped that would force the *Canadiens* to give up their French language and customs. In 1841, Upper and Lower Canada were united as the Province of Canada. Lower Canada was renamed Canada East, and Upper Canada was renamed Canada West.

In 1837, *Canadien* rebels encountered British troops at St. Eustache. Who do you think won this battle? What message does the picture give you?

The Fathers of Confederation negotiated the terms of the union of Canada East, Canada West, New Brunswick, and Nova Scotia at the Quebec Conference in 1864. Finally, on July 1, 1867, they became the first provinces in the new Dominion of Canada.

CONFEDERATION, 1867

Protection of French-Canadian rights and culture was a major issue when the leaders of Canada East, Canada West, New Brunswick, and Nova Scotia negotiated a union, or Confederation, in 1864. French-speaking supporters of the union convinced the people of Canada East that Confederation would preserve their old way of life. Opponents of the Confederation plan argued that union of three English-speaking provinces with one French-speaking province was all part of Lord Durham's program to

Louis Riel (centre) and the provisional government of Red River in 1869. How does this photograph compare to the one of the Fathers of Confederation? How would a photo of the Canadian government today be different from either of these group portraits?

erase *Canadien* culture. In the end, the voices for Confederation won, and Quebec became a province of Canada when the new country was born on July 1, 1867.

REBELLIONS IN THE WEST

In 1869, the battle for the rights of French-speaking people moved to present-day Manitoba. The French-speaking **Métis** of Red River, led by Louis Riel, demanded that Canada recognize their property, language, and education rights. In 1870, the Canadian government agreed, and Manitoba became the fifth province.

In 1885, Riel demanded similar rights for the Métis in present-day Saskatchewan. The Métis and Cree fought Canadian forces, and at the end of the rebellion, Riel was hanged for treason. People in Quebec considered Riel a hero and defender of their rights. People in English Canada called him a traitor. In 1890, Riel's native province of Manitoba abolished the French language in its schools and government. Many French Canadians saw these events as examples of how they were still considered a conquered people in Canada.

TENSIONS IN THE EARLY TWENTIETH CENTURY

In the early years of the twentieth century, French and English Canadians disagreed on major national questions. The Canadian government wanted to build a navy to help Britain if it went to war. English Canadians supported the idea. French Canadians were opposed, fearing their sons and daughters would be forced to fight Britain's wars in other parts of the world. Then, Ontario passed regulation to restrict the use of French in schools. For French Canadians, this was another step in Lord Durham's plan to erase the French culture from Canada.

During the First World War, which started in 1914, there was a shortage of soldiers, and English Canadians began calling for conscription that would force French Canadians into the war effort. The people of Quebec felt that the war in Europe had nothing to do with them. There were riots in the streets of Montreal and Quebec City against the Canadian government and the Canadian military. One member of the Quebec legislature suggested that Quebec should leave Confederation.

Examine these two posters from the First World War. What message does each give about conscription? What does each poster tell you about French and English views about the war?

THE QUIET REVOLUTION

When the Second World War ended in 1945, there were few tensions between French and English Canadians. However, by the end of the 1950s, Quebec was changing. The new leaders of the province introduced major changes in the schools and economy. These changes encouraged Quebeckers to appreciate their culture. Some young people expressed their pride through music, poetry, and writing. A few began to suggest that Quebec should become a country of its own. In 1967, their dream received support from the president of France, Charles de Gaulle. On a visit to Montreal, the president uttered the unforgettable words: "Vive le Québec libre!" ("Long live an independent Quebec!"). Many people in Quebec were inspired by the president's speech and began to support the idea of independence.

The slogan of the 1962 provincial election campaign in Quebec was "Maîtres chez nous" or "Masters in our own house." It symbolized the spirit of change sweeping French Canada. What do you think the expression means?

The October Crisis, 1970

In October 1970, a group of young French Canadians belonging to the FLQ, the Front de Libération du Québec, was determined to use violence to make Quebec an independent, French-speaking country. Members of the FLQ wanted to put an end to what they saw as the result of the British conquest of Canada: a country where French Canadians were poor and did hard manual labour, while many English Canadians were well paid as managers and owners of businesses. The FLQ robbed banks, set off explosives in Canadian government buildings, and kidnapped two men: James Cross, a British diplomat in Montreal, and Pierre Laporte, a minister in the Quebec government. They assassinated Laporte. FLQ members were tried and convicted of kidnapping and murder.

From October to December 1970, the Canadian army remained in Montreal to try to keep the peace during the October Crisis.

The Parti Québécois

The Parti Québécois, a new provincial party, was formed to fulfill the dream of many French Canadians for an independent country. In 1976, it won the provincial election and promised to end English domination of Quebec. As part of its program, the new government moved quickly to introduce Bill 101, which made French the official language of Quebec. The Bill also stated that all signs in the province would be in French only and that immigrants had to send their children to French schools. French-Canadian nationalists believed that the Bill would help to preserve Quebec culture and the French language.

"The most urgent task was, so to speak, to decolonize ourselves day by day, proving to ourselves and to others we were as capable as anyone of running our own affairs …"
—René Lévesque

From looking at this photograph, how divided do you think the people of Quebec were during the referendums?

REFERENDUMS FOR INDEPENDENCE

In 1980, the Parti Québécois held a **referendum** on the issue of Quebec sovereignty. In the referendum, all the people in the province were given the chance to cast a vote about Quebec's future. A "Oui" vote meant they wanted Quebec to separate from Canada and become independent. A "Non" vote" was a vote against Quebec separation. The result of the referendum was 60 per cent against separation and 40 per cent for separation.

Following this referendum result, Prime Minister Pierre Trudeau decided to change the Canadian **Constitution**. The process created more tensions between the French and English in Canada, because Quebec could not agree on many of the issues supported by the other provinces. Trudeau moved ahead with the constitutional changes without Quebec's approval, which created a deep rift between English and French Canadians. In 1982, Canada's new Constitution was signed.

In 1995, Quebec held a second referendum on the issue of separation. This time, the vote was very close. Just over 50 per cent of Quebec voters chose to keep the province as part of Canada. Today, many Quebeckers still dream of reversing the British conquest of North America by separating from Canada and changing our country forever.

◄ Playback ►

1. **Give examples of how different governments throughout our history have tried to protect or hurt the French language and culture.**

2. **In your opinion, should language and culture evolve naturally or should governments interfere in language and cultural issues?**

3. **The three themes of this book are conflict, change, and continuity. Based on your knowledge and understanding of the nature of the relationship between the French and English in Canada, suggest one change and one continuity you would like to see that would avoid future conflict between these two groups.**

The Back Story

Conflict, change, and continuity have been constant themes in Canadian history. They have shaped Canada and still define it. In this book, you have read about the conflicts between different groups and people, the changes brought about by the conflicts, and the aspects of life in Canada that have stayed constant over time.

The Goal

In a group of four, create a board game that charts the conflicts, changes, and continuity that you have read about in this book. Each game needs to include:

a) functional and creative packaging

b) a creative board game that reflects the theme of this book and that more than two people can play

c) game pieces that are appropriate to the theme

d) questions that reflect the information on conflict, change, and continuity presented in this book

e) detailed, concise, and easy-to-follow rules and procedures.

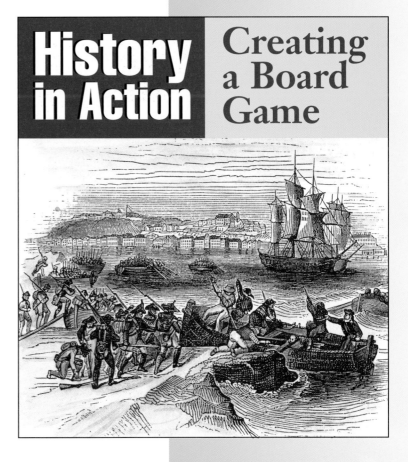

History in Action **Creating a Board Game**

The Steps

1. As a group, decide on the rules and procedures of your game.
2. Identify the tasks the group needs to do and assign them so that each member of the group creates a different part of the board game. Each group member must also contribute questions.
3. Present your board game to the class, explaining the choice of design, box, game pieces, rules, and procedures. After the presentation, you and your classmates will play all of the games.
4. Individually, write and submit to your teacher a paragraph explaining why it is important for students of Canadian history to play this game.

Evaluating Your Work

Think about these criteria as you complete your work. Your work should:

- reflect collaboration among group members, including respecting ideas and meeting deadlines
- include a box, board, and pieces that appropriately reflect all three themes: conflict, change, and continuity
- include questions that reflect these themes
- have a name that reflects the themes
- be attractive, neat, and complete
- include a paragraph, edited and with a topic sentence, supporting evidence, and closing sentence, explaining clearly why a student would benefit from playing this game.

Glossary

Acadians French-speaking people from Canada's Atlantic coast region who were driven off their land by the British in 1755 after they refused to take an oath of loyalty to the Protestant king of Great Britain. Thousands became refugees and fled to the American colonies, France, and New France.

Allies Nations or peoples who unite or join together for common goals, especially during wartime.

Antipathy An intense dislike.

Assembly A meeting of representatives elected by the people to debate issues, to make decisions, and to vote and pass laws.

Bilingual Having or speaking two languages, such as English and French, the two official languages of Canada.

Black powder An early form of gunpowder used in muskets.

Canadiens The name used for the original French-speaking settlers of New France.

Conquest Bringing an enemy people or country under control.

Constitution A document that lists the rules and regulations for the operation of a country, its governments, and its method of passing laws. Canada's constitution lists the specific powers for which the national and provincial governments are responsible.

Coureurs de bois Young French men who lived with the Native peoples, learned their languages, and made friendships in order to expand the fur trade.

Court-martialled When a soldier is put on trial before military judges.

Deportation A government act that forces a person or people to leave the country where they are residents.

Frontier The land between an area of settlement (where there are houses) and the wilderness.

Habitants The farmers of New France. Once a year, the *habitants* paid a special rent to their landlords, and were expected to pay a tax to the church.

Indulge To grant a wish, a privilege, or a right.

King's Road The main road, through Trois-Rivières, from Montreal to Quebec City.

La petite guerre A Native style of warfare where small groups of warriors launched surprise attacks on their enemies.

Louisbourg An important French fort at the mouth of the Gulf of St. Lawrence. It controlled important shipping in and out of the St. Lawrence River, the only route into New France.

Loyalist An American settler who remained loyal to Britain and the king during the American Revolution.

Métis People of mixed European (French or Scottish) and Native blood.

Muskets An early gun resembling a rifle that required a flint stone in order to fire it. Muskets fired lead balls rather than bullets.

Petition A written document that makes a request or statement, such as protesting an important decision or requesting legal rights.

Plains of Abraham The famous battle where the British under General Wolfe defeated the French under General Montcalm. This victory signalled an end to French control in North America.

Referendum A vote on a special question, such as Quebec independence, where all eligible voters have a say in the decision.

Rheumatism An illness that causes pain and swelling in a person's joints.

Seigneurs Privileged landlords who also served as military leaders in New France. They organized the *habitant* farmers into an army and led them during times of war.

Seniority The status a person earns by the number of years of service given to an army or a business.

Sentries Soldiers who watch for enemy attack.

Siege A military strategy of surrounding and attacking a fort or city to force the enemy into surrendering.

Tuberculosis A contagious disease that affects a person's lungs in particular.

Volley When a line of soldiers fire their guns at the same time, sending a hail of bullets at enemy lines.

Index

Credits

Reviewers

Cover top: *The Death of Wolfe*, by Benjamin West, National Gallery of Canada; bottom left: CBC, *Canada: A People's History*; bottom right: CP/Ryan Remiorz; Page 1 Library and Archives Canada, C-001078; Page 2 top right: Library and Archives Canada, C-016951; top left: Mary Evans Picture Library; bottom: The Granger Collection; Page 3 top left: Library and Archives Canada, C-040575; middle: The Granger Collection; right: Mary Evans Picture Library; Library and Archives Canada, C-016951; Page 4 Mary Evans Picture Library; Page 5 map, Paperglyphs; Page 6 The Arms of Canada has been reproduced with the permission of the Government of Canada; Page 7 map, Paperglyphs; Page 8 *The Horse Trader*, Cornelius Krieghoff, The Beaverbrook Gallery; Page 9 *Indian Hunters*, 1867, Cornelius Krieghoff, The Beaverbrook Gallery; Page 10 *Coming Storm at the Portage*, 1859, Cornelius Krieghoff, The Beaverbrook Gallery; Page 11 Library and Archives Canada, Acc. No. 1990-553-1190; Page 12 map, Paperglyphs; Page 13 Musée acadien, Université de Moncton; Page 14 map, Paperglyphs; Page 15 After C. Schuessele/National Archives of Canada, C-002644; Page 16 Library and Archives Canada, Acc. No. 1991-209-1; Page 17 Library and Archives Canada, Acc. No. 1970-188-497; Page 18 Library and Archives Canada, C-020464/C7111; Page 19 CBC, *Canada: A People's History*; Page 20 Mary Evans Picture Library; Page 21 Library and Archives Canada, Acc. No. 1972-26-1382; Page 22 Library and Archives of Canada/C-43483; Page 23 CBC, *Canada: A People's History*; Page 24 Library and Archives of Canada, Acc. No. R9266-1388 Peter Winkworth Collection of Canadiana; Page 25 Library and Archives of Canada, Acc. No. 1991-19-1; Page 26 Canadian Military College; Page 28 Library and Archives of Canada/C-77769; Page 29 Library and Archives of Canada, Acc. No. 1993-326-1; Page 30 The Granger Collection: Page 31 Library and Archives Canada; Page 32 *The Death of Wolfe*, Benjamin West, National Gallery of Canada; Page 33 Library and Archives of Canada, Acc. No. 1992-486-1; Page 34 Library and Archives of Canada, Acc. No. 1972-26-1382; Page 35 Library and Archives of Canada, Acc. No. 1989-518-15; Page 36 Library and Archives of Canada, Acc. No. 1989-283-11; Page 37 Mary Evans Picture Library; Page 38 Library and Archives of Canada, C-11043; Page 39 Library and Archives of Canada, NMC21404; Page 40 The Granger Collection; Page 41 Library and Archives Canada, Acc. No, 1958-214-1; Page 42 Library and Archives Canada, Acc. No. 1997-227-1; Page 43 map, Paperglyphs; Page 44 Library and Archives Canada online; Page 45 Library and Archives Canada; Page 46 Library and Archives Canada, Acc. No. 1997-8-1; Page 47 Library and Archives Canada, Acc. No. 1989-218-5; Page 48 The Granger Collection; Page 49 The Granger Collection; Page 50 map, Paperglyphs; Page 51 Library of Congress Prints and Photographs Division Washington, D.C. 20540 USA; Page 52 map, Paperglyphs; Page 53 the Granger Collection; Page 55 Mary Evans Picture Library; Page 56 map, Paperglyphs; Page 57 CP/Ryan Remiorz; Page 58 top left: Library and Archives, PA-012854; right: Library and Archives Canada, Acc. No. 1992-566-6; bottom: map, Paperglyphs; Page 59 top left: CP/Journal de Quebec; right: CP/Ryan Remiorz; bottom Library and Archives Canada, C-000396; Page 60 top: House of Commons; bottom: Library and Archives Canada, PA-012854; Page 61 top: Library and Archives Canada, Acc. No. 1983-28-776; bottom: Library and Archives Canada, Acc. No. 1983-28-897; Page 62 Montreal Gazette Photo Collection; Page 63 top: CP/Journal de Quebec; bottom: CP/Montreal Star; Page 64 CP Photo Archive; Page 65 The Granger Collection.

Kathryn Brownell, Terry Fox School, Toronto, Ontario

Manny Calisto, West St. Paul School, West St. Paul, Manitoba

Greer Coe, Montague Intermediate School, Montague, Prince Edward Island

Rick Elliott, John Buchan School, Toronto, Ontario

Sheri Epstein, Langstaff High School, Thornhill, Ontario

Christine Greene, Avalon East School Board, St. John's, Newfoundland

Joanne Wheeler, St. Margaret School, Calgary, Alberta